The History o

The Hidden G
Pyrenees

Copyright © 2023 by Nuria Rehn and Einar Felix Hansen.

All rights reserved. No part of this publication may be reproduced, stored in a retrieval system, or transmitted, in any form or by any means, electronic, mechanical, photocopying, recording, or otherwise, without the prior written permission of the copyright holder. This book was created with the help of Artificial Intelligence technology.

The contents of this book are intended for entertainment purposes only. While every effort has been made to ensure the accuracy and reliability of the information presented, the author and publisher make no warranties or representations as to the accuracy, completeness, or suitability of the information contained herein. The information presented in this book is not intended as a substitute for professional advice, and readers should consult with qualified professionals in the relevant fields for specific advice.

The Land of the Pyrenees: An Introduction to Andorra 6

Prehistoric Andorra: Tracing the Origins 11

Roman Influence: Andorra during Antiquity 16

Visigothic Rule and the Dark Ages 19

Charlemagne's Influence: Andorra in the Carolingian Empire 22

Feudal Beginnings: Andorra's Emergence as a Sovereign State 25

Andorra's Unique Co-Principality: The Origins of a Dual Governance System 28

The Role of the Bishop of Urgell: Ecclesiastical Influence in Andorra 31

The Count of Foix and the Birth of the Co-Principality 34

The Consolidation of Andorra's Political Structure 37

Feudalism and Land Tenure in Medieval Andorra 40

Andorra in the Reconquista: A Buffer Zone between Christians and Muslims 43

Challenging Times: Andorra in the Hundred Years' War 46

Border Disputes and the Impact on Andorra's Sovereignty 49

The Influence of the Catholic Church in Medieval Andorra 52

Trade and Commerce in Medieval Andorra 55

The Catalan-Aragonese Union and Andorra 58

Andorra and the Kingdom of France: The Treaty of Corbeil 61

The War of the Spanish Succession and its Effect on Andorra 64

The Age of Enlightenment and Andorra's Intellectual Awakening 67

Andorra's Resilience: Surviving the Napoleonic Era 70

Andorra in the 20th Century: From Agrarian Society to Tourism Hub 74

Contemporary Andorra: Economy, Society, and Governance 79

The Cultural Heritage of Andorra: Preserving Tradition in a Modern World 84

Andorra: A Country of the Past and the Future 89

The Land of the Pyrenees: An Introduction to Andorra

Nestled in the heart of the Pyrenees, Andorra is a small landlocked country renowned for its stunning natural beauty and rich history. This chapter serves as an in-depth introduction to Andorra, exploring its geographical features, climate, and the unique characteristics that have shaped its development.

Geographically, Andorra is located in southwestern Europe, sharing borders with Spain to the south and France to the north. With an area of approximately 468 square kilometers (181 square miles), it is one of the smallest countries on the continent. Its strategic position in the eastern Pyrenees Mountains has played a significant role in its history, contributing to its distinct cultural and political identity.

The Pyrenees, a majestic mountain range stretching approximately 430 kilometers (267 miles) between the Atlantic Ocean and the Mediterranean Sea, dominate the landscape of Andorra. This rugged terrain boasts peaks reaching over 2,900 meters (9,500 feet) in elevation, with Coma Pedrosa standing as the highest point in the country at 2,942 meters (9,652 feet). The mountains not only provide a stunning backdrop but also serve as a natural barrier, isolating Andorra from its neighboring countries and contributing to its unique development.

The climate of Andorra is largely influenced by its mountainous setting. Its high elevation and proximity to the Mediterranean Sea result in a temperate climate with distinct seasonal variations. Winters are typically cold and snowy, with temperatures frequently dropping below freezing. The mountain peaks are often blanketed in snow, attracting winter sports enthusiasts from around the world. Summers are mild and pleasant, with temperatures averaging around 20 to 25 degrees Celsius (68 to 77 degrees Fahrenheit). The region experiences a significant amount of rainfall throughout the year, contributing to the lush green valleys and alpine meadows that dot the landscape.

Throughout its history, Andorra has managed to preserve its independence and unique political structure. It is a parliamentary co-principality, meaning it is jointly ruled by two co-princes: the Bishop of Urgell, a Spanish prelate, and the President of France. This unusual arrangement dates back to the Middle Ages and is a testament to the complex historical and cultural influences that have shaped Andorra.

Archaeological evidence suggests that human habitation in the region dates back to the Neolithic period, with traces of early settlements and megalithic structures discovered. The influence of the Roman Empire is evident in Andorra, as it was a vital crossroad connecting the provinces of Hispania and Gallia. Roman artifacts, including coins and pottery, have been unearthed, indicating a significant Roman presence in the area.

During the early medieval period, Andorra found itself caught in the power struggles between the Muslim Moors and the Christian kingdoms of the Iberian Peninsula. The region became a buffer zone between the two forces, with fortifications and watchtowers erected to protect against invasions. It was during this time that the establishment of a co-principality began to take shape, with the Count of Urgell and the Count of Foix asserting their authority over the land.

By the 13th century, a charter was granted to Andorra by the Count of Foix, Gaston VII. This charter, known as the Pareatges, outlined the rights and responsibilities of the co-princes, as well as the local population. The Pareatges served as the foundation for Andorra's unique governance system, combining feudal and democratic elements that continue to shape the country's political structure today.

Andorra's mountainous terrain, with its challenging passes and rugged landscapes, has traditionally isolated the country from external influences. This geographical seclusion allowed Andorra to develop its own distinct customs, traditions, and way of life. It also contributed to the formation of a resilient and self-sufficient society, as the inhabitants adapted to the harsh conditions of the mountains.

The history of Andorra is closely intertwined with the neighboring regions of Catalonia and Occitania. Over the centuries, Andorra found itself at the crossroads of political and cultural influences from these areas. The Counts of Urgell, who held authority over Andorra, maintained close ties with the Counts of Barcelona and the Kingdom of Aragon. This connection solidified the Catalan influence in the region, shaping Andorra's language, culture, and legal system.

During the Middle Ages, Andorra faced numerous challenges as power dynamics shifted in the region. Border disputes between neighboring lords, kingdoms, and ecclesiastical authorities often put Andorra in the midst of conflicts. The co-princes, the Bishop of Urgell and the Count of Foix, exerted their authority over Andorra, leading to periods of tension and negotiation. These power struggles, however, ultimately contributed to the establishment of a unique co-principality that has endured to this day.

In addition to its political history, Andorra boasts a rich cultural heritage. The art, architecture, and folklore of the region are deeply rooted in its medieval origins. Romanesque churches and chapels dot the landscape, showcasing the artistic and architectural achievements of the time. The iconic Sant Joan de Caselles and Santa Coloma churches are excellent examples of this distinctive style.

The economy of medieval Andorra relied heavily on agriculture, livestock farming, and trade. The fertile valleys and mountain pastures provided resources for sustenance, while trade routes passing through Andorra connected the markets of Catalonia, Occitania, and beyond. The exchange of goods and ideas enriched the region, contributing to its cultural diversity and prosperity.

As time progressed, Andorra experienced significant changes brought about by external forces, such as the War of the Spanish Succession and the Napoleonic Wars. These conflicts challenged the country's independence and led to brief periods of foreign occupation. However, the resilience of the Andorran people and their commitment to their unique governance system allowed the country to weather these storms and maintain its autonomy.

In more recent times, Andorra has embraced its natural beauty and developed a thriving tourism industry. The pristine mountain landscapes, with their hiking trails, ski resorts, and adventure sports opportunities, attract visitors from around the world. The country's commitment to environmental preservation and sustainable tourism practices ensures that future generations can continue to appreciate and enjoy its natural treasures.

Andorra's history is as fascinating as its breathtaking landscapes. From its ancient origins to the challenges of medieval power struggles and its remarkable governance structure, Andorra stands as a testament to the enduring spirit of a nation nestled in the Pyrenees. Its cultural heritage, traditions, and natural beauty make it a truly captivating destination, inviting exploration and appreciation for its remarkable past and present.

Prehistoric Andorra: Tracing the Origins

In the remote corners of Andorra's history, beyond the annals of recorded civilization, lies a period known as prehistoric Andorra. This chapter delves into the enigmatic beginnings of human habitation in the region, tracing the origins of Andorra's prehistoric past.

The origins of human presence in Andorra can be traced back to the Paleolithic era, a time characterized by the use of stone tools and the development of early hunting and gathering societies. Archaeological evidence suggests that the earliest inhabitants of Andorra were nomadic groups who traversed the Pyrenees, following the migratory patterns of animals and utilizing the region's resources for their survival.

Excavations conducted in various locations across Andorra have uncovered important remnants from this era. Stone tools, such as hand axes, scrapers, and blades, have been found, indicating the early inhabitants' skills in crafting tools for hunting, butchering, and other essential activities. These tools provide valuable insights into the daily lives and survival strategies of the prehistoric Andorran communities.

As the climate fluctuated over the millennia, transitioning between cold glacial periods and warmer interglacial periods, the landscape of Andorra underwent significant changes. During the last glacial maximum, which occurred approximately 20,000 years ago, much of the region was covered by ice and snow. However, as the ice receded during the subsequent millennia, plant and animal life gradually returned, creating favorable conditions for human habitation.

With the onset of the Neolithic period around 6,000 BCE, a fundamental shift occurred in human societies worldwide, including Andorra. During this period, humans transitioned from a nomadic lifestyle to a more settled existence based on agriculture and the domestication of animals. In Andorra, this transition brought about substantial changes in the social, economic, and cultural fabric of prehistoric communities.

Evidence of Neolithic settlement in Andorra can be found in the form of megalithic structures and dolmens. These megalithic monuments, constructed using large stones, served various purposes, such as burial sites or ceremonial spaces. The presence of these structures indicates the emergence of social organization, religious beliefs, and the establishment of more permanent settlements.

The Neolithic inhabitants of Andorra engaged in subsistence activities such as farming and animal husbandry. Archaeological excavations have uncovered traces of ancient cultivated fields, suggesting the cultivation of crops like wheat, barley, and legumes. Domesticated animals, including sheep, goats, and cattle, were also an essential part of their agricultural practices. The ability to sustain themselves through farming and herding laid the foundation for more settled communities and the development of social hierarchies.

In addition to agriculture, prehistoric Andorrans utilized the region's natural resources for their daily needs.

Forests provided timber for construction, fuel, and materials for toolmaking. The rivers and streams offered a source of freshwater, as well as fish and other aquatic resources. Andorra's mountainous terrain presented opportunities for hunting game, gathering wild plants, and the exploitation of mineral resources such as copper, which played a crucial role in tool production.

The knowledge and skills acquired by prehistoric Andorrans were likely transmitted through oral traditions, as no written records from this period have been discovered. However, the material artifacts left behind provide glimpses into their craftsmanship and artistic expression. Decorated ceramics, stone carvings, and personal adornments like beads and pendants reveal the creativity and cultural expressions of these ancient communities.

It is important to note that our understanding of prehistoric Andorra is continually evolving as new discoveries are made and archaeological techniques advance. Each excavation and analysis adds a layer of knowledge, shedding light on the daily lives, beliefs, and interactions of the prehistoric Andorrans. However, it is essential to approach the interpretation of these findings with caution, as the absence of written records makes it challenging to fully comprehend the complexities of their societies.

While the exact ethnic and linguistic identities of the prehistoric Andorrans remain elusive, it is believed that they belonged to broader cultural groups that inhabited the surrounding regions. The influences of neighboring cultures, such as the Iberians and the early Celts, may have played a role in shaping their traditions and practices.

As time progressed, the influence of external cultures began to seep into Andorra. With the arrival of the Bronze Age around 2000 BCE, advancements in metallurgy brought about significant changes in the material culture of the region. Bronze tools, weapons, and ornaments replaced their stone counterparts, highlighting the increasing sophistication of craftsmanship and trade networks.

The Iron Age further transformed prehistoric Andorra. Iron, more abundant and durable than bronze, became the preferred metal for toolmaking and weapon production. The increased efficiency and productivity associated with ironworking had profound implications for the development of Andorran society, facilitating agricultural expansion, trade, and specialization of labor.

The prehistoric era in Andorra came to a close with the arrival of the Roman Empire in the Iberian Peninsula. Around the 2nd century BCE, the Romans began their conquest and colonization of the region, introducing new political, social, and economic structures. Andorra, located on the periphery of the empire, likely experienced some level of Roman influence, although the extent of direct Roman presence and administration in the region remains uncertain.

In conclusion, the origins of Andorra can be traced back to prehistoric times when early human communities roamed the Pyrenean landscape, adapting to the challenges and opportunities presented by their environment. From the nomadic lifestyles of the

Paleolithic era to the settled agricultural communities of the Neolithic and the advancements of the Bronze and Iron Ages, prehistoric Andorra underwent significant transformations. While our knowledge of this period is limited, archaeological evidence provides valuable glimpses into the lives, cultural practices, and technological advancements of the prehistoric Andorrans. The ongoing exploration and study of this era continue to shed light on the ancient origins of this remarkable land in the Pyrenees.

Roman Influence: Andorra during Antiquity

The period of Roman influence marks a significant chapter in the history of Andorra, as the Roman Empire expanded its dominion into the Iberian Peninsula. This chapter delves into the impact of Roman presence on Andorra during antiquity, examining the cultural, social, and economic transformations brought about by Roman rule.

During the late 3rd century BCE, the Roman Republic initiated its conquest of the Iberian Peninsula, known as Hispania. As the Romans expanded their territorial control, the Pyrenees Mountains, including the region that would become Andorra, stood as a natural barrier separating the Romanized territories to the south from the non-Romanized areas to the north.

The exact extent of direct Roman administration and influence in Andorra remains uncertain. While there is a lack of conclusive evidence pointing to a significant Roman presence within the borders of present-day Andorra, it is believed that the region experienced some level of Roman influence, primarily through cultural, economic, and political interactions.

Roman roads played a vital role in connecting the various parts of the empire, facilitating trade, and enabling the movement of troops. The Via Augusta, a major Roman road, stretched from Rome through Hispania, passing near Andorra. This road likely served as a vital artery for communication and commerce, contributing to the integration of Andorra into the wider Roman networks.

The proximity of Andorra to Romanized regions in Hispania and Gaul presented opportunities for cultural exchange and trade. The indigenous communities of Andorra would have had contact with Roman settlers and traders, exposing them to Roman customs, language, and material culture. This influence is visible in the archaeological findings, such as Roman coins and pottery, discovered in the region, indicating economic interactions and the presence of Roman goods.

One significant aspect of Roman influence was the spread of Latin, the language of the Roman Empire. It is likely that Latin had an impact on the linguistic landscape of Andorra, particularly in areas with closer ties to Romanized regions. However, the precise extent and nature of this linguistic influence are challenging to determine due to the limited available evidence.

The Roman Empire brought with it a system of governance and administration that had a profound impact on the surrounding regions. While the exact administrative organization of Andorra during Roman times is uncertain, it is plausible that the region fell under the jurisdiction of nearby Romanized territories. Roman legal and administrative practices, including the establishment of municipal governments, may have influenced local governance structures in Andorra.

Religion also underwent changes during the Roman period. The Roman pantheon of gods and goddesses, with its own distinct mythology and rituals, likely coexisted with local indigenous beliefs and practices. The spread of

Roman religious practices may have left traces in the religious landscape of Andorra, although the specific details are largely speculative due to the scarcity of evidence.

The Roman period in Andorra came to an end with the decline and fall of the Western Roman Empire in the 5th century CE. The subsequent centuries witnessed a shifting power dynamic in the region, with various Visigothic and Moorish invasions and settlements.

In conclusion, the impact of Roman influence on Andorra during antiquity is evident in the cultural, economic, and social spheres. While the precise nature and extent of Roman administration in Andorra remain uncertain, the presence of Roman roads, material culture, and potential linguistic and religious influences point to connections and interactions between the indigenous communities and the wider Roman world. The legacy of Roman influence in Andorra serves as a testament to the enduring significance of the Roman Empire in shaping the historical narrative of the region.

Visigothic Rule and the Dark Ages

The period following the decline of the Roman Empire in the Western Mediterranean, often referred to as the Dark Ages, witnessed a series of political and social upheavals. This chapter explores the era of Visigothic rule in the Iberian Peninsula and its implications for Andorra. It delves into the political dynamics, cultural influences, and the overall historical context of this transformative period.

With the decline of Roman authority in the 5th century CE, the Visigoths, a Germanic tribe originating from Central Europe, seized the opportunity to establish their own kingdom in the Iberian Peninsula. Their influence extended over vast territories, including present-day Andorra, and marked a significant shift in the regional power structure.

The Visigoths, under their king, Euric, expanded their kingdom and solidified their rule throughout the Iberian Peninsula. However, the precise extent of their control over Andorra is challenging to ascertain due to the limited historical records from this period. It is likely that Andorra, situated in the northeastern corner of the peninsula, fell under the broader Visigothic administration.

Visigothic rule brought about notable changes in the social, cultural, and religious fabric of the region. The Visigoths were adherents of Arianism, a Christian doctrine considered heretical by the Roman Catholic Church. Their religious beliefs diverged from those of the Roman Catholic population in the area, and this religious disparity may have contributed to social tensions and conflicts.

During the Visigothic era, the Christian Church played a pivotal role in society, serving as a unifying force and a center of power. The conversion of the Visigoths to Catholicism in the late 6th century CE, under the rule of King Reccared I, marked a significant shift in religious dynamics. This conversion had implications for the religious landscape of Andorra, potentially bringing it into closer alignment with Catholic practices.

While the Visigoths maintained a semblance of Roman-influenced governance, their rule was not without challenges. Internal conflicts and external pressures, including invasions by the Byzantine Empire and the Islamic Moors, gradually weakened the Visigothic kingdom. These factors set the stage for the subsequent Arab conquest of the Iberian Peninsula.

The arrival of the Moors in the early 8th century CE marked a turning point in the history of the Iberian Peninsula, including Andorra. The Moorish conquest brought about significant changes, with the region falling under Islamic rule for several centuries. However, due to its remote and mountainous location, Andorra experienced limited direct Arab influence compared to other parts of the peninsula.

The precise historical details of this period, often referred to as the Dark Ages, are challenging to unravel due to the scarcity of written records. The lack of substantial archaeological evidence further complicates our understanding of the specific events and societal developments during this time. Nevertheless, it is reasonable to infer that Andorra, situated on the periphery of the broader political and cultural shifts, experienced a degree of isolation from the major historical currents of the era.

In conclusion, the era of Visigothic rule in the Iberian Peninsula and the subsequent Dark Ages were characterized by political instability, religious transformations, and societal transitions. The precise impact of Visigothic rule on Andorra remains challenging to determine due to the limited available historical sources. However, the emergence of the Visigothic kingdom, its religious policies, and the subsequent arrival of the Moors set the stage for the complex historical narrative that would unfold in the centuries to come. The Dark Ages provide a backdrop of uncertainty and change, laying the groundwork for the evolving identity and history of Andorra.

Charlemagne's Influence: Andorra in the Carolingian Empire

The period of Charlemagne's reign in the 8th and 9th centuries marked a significant chapter in European history, including the region that would become Andorra. This chapter explores Charlemagne's influence on Andorra within the broader context of the Carolingian Empire. It delves into the political, cultural, and socio-economic dynamics of the era, shedding light on the lasting impact of Charlemagne's rule.

Charlemagne, also known as Charles the Great, was the King of the Franks and Lombards, and his reign laid the foundation for the Carolingian Empire. Charlemagne's ambitious military campaigns and his vision of a unified Christian empire brought him into contact with the Pyrenean region, including Andorra.

The precise details of Charlemagne's direct influence on Andorra are challenging to ascertain due to the scarcity of historical records from this period. However, it is plausible to infer that Andorra fell under the sphere of Carolingian authority, given its geographical location within the broader Carolingian dominion.

One significant aspect of Charlemagne's reign was his interest in governance and administration. He sought to establish a centralized system of rule, appointing officials known as counts to oversee various territories. These counts were responsible for enforcing Carolingian policies, collecting taxes, and maintaining order.

The counts appointed by Charlemagne likely held authority over the Pyrenean region, including Andorra. Their role would have involved managing local affairs, representing the Carolingian empire's interests, and ensuring the collection of tribute or taxes from the inhabitants of Andorra.

Charlemagne's reign also saw a renewed emphasis on Christianity and the spread of the Catholic Church's influence. As a devout Christian ruler, Charlemagne actively promoted the Christian faith, often by forceful means. The Christianization of the region, including Andorra, was an integral part of the Carolingian agenda, with efforts focused on converting the local population to Catholicism.

The establishment of monastic communities played a significant role in the spread of Christianity and the promotion of learning and culture. Monasteries served as centers of religious and intellectual life, preserving and disseminating knowledge. While there is limited evidence of monastic activity specifically in Andorra during this period, it is reasonable to assume that the influence of monastic institutions in the surrounding regions would have indirectly affected Andorra as well.

Trade and economic activities also experienced a degree of revitalization under Carolingian rule. Charlemagne sought to stimulate commerce and economic growth within his empire. The strategic location of Andorra, nestled between the Iberian Peninsula and the Frankish territories, would have made it a vital transit route for trade and travel.

It is plausible that Andorra served as a hub for the exchange of goods, linking the markets of the Mediterranean and the northern regions. This would have brought economic opportunities to the inhabitants of Andorra, facilitating the trade of agricultural products, textiles, and other commodities.

While the specific historical details of this period in Andorra's history may be elusive, the broader influences of Charlemagne's reign and the Carolingian Empire are evident in the political, religious, and economic spheres. The efforts to establish centralized governance, promote Christianity, and stimulate trade had lasting implications for the region and set the stage for future developments in Andorra.

In conclusion, Charlemagne's influence on Andorra during the Carolingian period was multifaceted, encompassing political administration, religious transformation, and economic activities. While the direct impact of Charlemagne's rule on Andorra may be difficult to discern, the broader dynamics of the Carolingian Empire undoubtedly shaped the trajectory of the region. The historical significance of this period is reflected in the enduring cultural and political legacies that emerged in Andorra and the surrounding regions.

Feudal Beginnings: Andorra's Emergence as a Sovereign State

The emergence of Andorra as a sovereign state during the feudal period represents a significant milestone in its history. This chapter delves into the intricacies of Andorra's feudal beginnings, examining the political, social, and economic factors that contributed to its unique status as a co-principality.

Feudalism, a system characterized by the exchange of land for service and loyalty, gained prominence in Europe during the Middle Ages. Andorra, situated in the Pyrenees Mountains, found itself at the intersection of competing feudal powers, setting the stage for the formation of its distinctive governance structure.

The precise origins of Andorra's co-principality can be traced back to the early medieval period, when various feudal lords asserted their influence over the region. Two primary figures emerged as co-princes: the Bishop of Urgell, representing the ecclesiastical authority, and the Count of Foix, representing the secular power.

The Bishop of Urgell, as a representative of the Catholic Church, held spiritual and temporal authority in the region. The count of Foix, on the other hand, belonged to the ruling dynasty of the County of Foix, a feudal territory neighboring Andorra. These co-princes jointly exercised sovereignty over Andorra, with their authority based on a series of historical agreements known as pareatges.

The pareatges, or co-principal agreement, served as the foundational documents for Andorra's unique governance system. The earliest known pareatge dates back to the 13th century, granted by the Count of Foix to the Bishop of Urgell. These agreements outlined the rights, responsibilities, and privileges of the co-princes, as well as the local population.

Under the co-principality, Andorra enjoyed a degree of autonomy and self-governance. The inhabitants of Andorra were granted certain rights and liberties, such as the ability to manage local affairs, administer justice, and collect taxes. These privileges were essential in fostering a sense of communal identity and solidarity among the Andorran people.

The co-princes, in turn, relied on the support and loyalty of the local population for the administration and defense of Andorra. The feudal relationship between the co-princes and the Andorran community was based on reciprocal obligations and mutual interests. The inhabitants provided military service and other forms of support to the co-princes in exchange for protection and the preservation of their rights.

The geographical characteristics of Andorra played a crucial role in shaping its feudal development. The mountainous terrain provided a natural defense, making it less vulnerable to external invasions and allowing the local population to maintain a certain level of independence. The isolation offered by the Pyrenees Mountains fostered a sense of self-sufficiency and self-governance, enabling Andorra to develop its own unique political and cultural identity.

Economically, Andorra relied on agriculture, animal husbandry, and trade to sustain its population. The fertile valleys and mountain pastures provided resources for farming and herding, while trade routes passing through Andorra facilitated the exchange of goods between the Iberian Peninsula and other European regions. This economic activity contributed to the prosperity of Andorra and its ability to maintain its autonomy within the feudal system.

Over the centuries, Andorra's co-principality evolved and adapted to changing political and social dynamics. While the specific historical details of this period may be scarce, the resilience and ingenuity of the Andorran people allowed them to navigate the challenges of feudalism and maintain their distinct political structure.

In conclusion, Andorra's emergence as a sovereign state during the feudal period was marked by the establishment of its co-principality. The co-princes, representing both ecclesiastical and secular authority, played a central role in governing Andorra through the pareatges. The co-principality granted a degree of autonomy to the Andorran people while ensuring the protection and administration of the region.

Andorra's Unique Co-Principality: The Origins of a Dual Governance System

Andorra's co-principality stands as a remarkable example of a dual governance system, where two entities share sovereignty over the land. This chapter explores the origins of Andorra's unique co-principality, delving into the historical circumstances and agreements that gave rise to this distinctive form of governance.

The foundations of Andorra's co-principality can be traced back to the medieval period, specifically to the 13th century. Historical records indicate that the first formal agreement between the Count of Foix and the Bishop of Urgell was established in 1278, solidifying their joint authority over Andorra.

The Count of Foix, as the secular co-prince, represented the political power in Andorra, while the Bishop of Urgell, as the ecclesiastical co-prince, represented the spiritual authority. This division of power between the secular and religious realms was a common feature of the feudal era.

The origins of the co-principality can be attributed to the complex geopolitical landscape of the Pyrenees during the Middle Ages. Andorra found itself situated between competing feudal powers, with the Kingdom of Aragon and the Crown of Castile exerting influence over the region. The co-principality provided a solution to the challenge of maintaining independence while navigating the power dynamics of the surrounding territories.

The earliest agreements between the Count of Foix and the Bishop of Urgell, known as the pareatges, established the rights, responsibilities, and privileges of both co-princes. These agreements outlined the shared governance and administration of Andorra, ensuring a balance of power between the secular and ecclesiastical authorities.

The pareatges defined various aspects of governance, including matters of justice, taxation, and defense. They also addressed the roles and functions of the co-princes, as well as the rights and obligations of the Andorran population. These agreements provided a framework for the unique dual governance system that continues to shape Andorra's political structure.

Under the co-principality, the co-princes held joint authority and shared the responsibilities of governance. They appointed local representatives, known as veguers, to oversee the administration of Andorra on their behalf. The veguers acted as officials who managed local affairs, collected taxes, and maintained order in accordance with the directives of the co-princes.

The Andorran people, known as the "paréage," played an active role in the co-principality. Their rights, privileges, and obligations were outlined in the pareatges, ensuring their participation in the governance of their land. The paréage enjoyed certain freedoms and communal rights, including the ability to participate in decision-making processes and the management of local affairs.

The co-princes relied on the support and loyalty of the Andorran population, and in return, the inhabitants received protection and the preservation of their rights.

This reciprocal relationship formed the foundation of the co-principality, fostering a sense of communal identity and shared responsibility for the well-being of Andorra.

The co-princes also maintained their own separate territories outside of Andorra. The Count of Foix held sway over the County of Foix, while the Bishop of Urgell governed the Diocese of Urgell. This separation of territories allowed the co-princes to balance their responsibilities and interests in Andorra while attending to their other domains.

The co-principality of Andorra endured through the centuries, adapting to changes in the political and social landscape. It weathered challenges, such as disputes over succession and territorial claims by neighboring powers. The co-princes and the Andorran people navigated these challenges through diplomacy, negotiations, and the preservation of their shared governance structure.

In conclusion, Andorra's co-principality, with its dual governance system, has its origins in the medieval period, specifically in the 13th century. The division of power between the Count of Foix and the Bishop of Urgell created a unique arrangement where secular and ecclesiastical authorities shared sovereignty over Andorra.

The Role of the Bishop of Urgell: Ecclesiastical Influence in Andorra

The Bishop of Urgell has played a significant role in the governance and religious life of Andorra throughout its history. This chapter explores the ecclesiastical influence of the Bishop of Urgell in Andorra, examining their role, responsibilities, and impact on the cultural and social fabric of the co-principality.

The Bishop of Urgell, as one of the co-princes of Andorra, represents the ecclesiastical authority within the dual governance system. The bishopric of Urgell, located in the historical region of Catalonia, has a long-standing history dating back to the early medieval period.

The role of the Bishop of Urgell in Andorra is multifaceted, encompassing both spiritual and temporal aspects. Ecclesiastically, the bishop holds jurisdiction over the religious matters of the region, overseeing the Catholic Church's presence and activities. The bishop plays a crucial role in preserving and promoting Catholicism in Andorra, fostering religious practices and ensuring the spiritual well-being of the population.

The ecclesiastical influence of the Bishop of Urgell is particularly evident in matters of religious administration. The bishop appoints priests to serve in the parishes of Andorra, ensuring the availability of religious services and pastoral care for the Andorran population. The bishop's authority also extends to matters of religious education, sacraments, and the maintenance of religious institutions.

The Bishop of Urgell's involvement in the co-principality's governance extends beyond religious affairs. As a co-prince, they hold joint authority over matters of justice, taxation, and defense, as outlined in the pareatges. The bishop appoints representatives, known as veguers, to manage the secular administration of Andorra on their behalf, ensuring the effective governance of the region.

The religious influence of the Bishop of Urgell is visible in the cultural and social fabric of Andorra. Catholicism has played a central role in shaping the religious traditions, customs, and celebrations of the Andorran people. The presence of Catholic churches, chapels, and religious artifacts throughout the co-principality bears witness to the enduring impact of the ecclesiastical authority.

The Bishop of Urgell's influence extends beyond religious matters and governance. They have traditionally held a position of respect and authority in the Andorran society. The bishop's involvement in ceremonial events, such as the inauguration of the co-princes, the coronation of the elected heads of government, and the blessing of important occasions, reinforces their symbolic and social significance.

Historically, the Bishop of Urgell has acted as a mediator and diplomat, representing Andorra's interests in external affairs. Their diplomatic role has been crucial in navigating the complex relationships with neighboring powers and ensuring the preservation of Andorra's autonomy within the broader geopolitical context.

The Bishop of Urgell's influence in Andorra has evolved over time, adapting to changing historical circumstances. The bishopric of Urgell has witnessed periods of expansion, consolidation, and challenges to its authority. Nevertheless, the bishop has maintained a consistent presence and involvement in the religious and secular affairs of Andorra.

In conclusion, the role of the Bishop of Urgell in Andorra's governance and religious life has been significant. As a co-prince, they represent the ecclesiastical authority within the dual governance system, overseeing religious administration, appointing representatives, and contributing to the secular governance of Andorra. The ecclesiastical influence of the Bishop of Urgell is evident in the religious traditions, cultural practices, and social fabric of the co-principality. Their role as a mediator and diplomat has been instrumental in preserving Andorra's autonomy within the broader geopolitical context.

The Count of Foix and the Birth of the Co-Principality

The Count of Foix played a crucial role in the establishment of the co-principality of Andorra, marking the birth of a unique dual governance system. This chapter delves into the historical context, the role of the Count of Foix, and the agreements that laid the foundation for the co-princeship in Andorra.

The Count of Foix, a prominent figure in the feudal landscape of the Pyrenees region, belonged to the ruling dynasty of the County of Foix, a territory situated in the historical region of Occitania. The Count of Foix wielded significant secular power and held authority over a domain neighboring Andorra.

The emergence of the co-princeship in Andorra can be traced back to the 13th century, a period marked by political realignments and territorial disputes in the Pyrenees. The precise circumstances leading to the involvement of the Count of Foix in Andorra's governance are not fully documented, but historical records suggest that the count's influence expanded into the region.

The birth of the co-princeship can be attributed to a series of agreements known as pareatges, which defined the rights, responsibilities, and privileges of the co-princes. The earliest recorded pareatge dates back to 1278, between the Count of Foix and the Bishop of Urgell. These agreements outlined the shared sovereignty over

Andorra, establishing the framework for the dual governance system.

The pareatges between the Count of Foix and the Bishop of Urgell granted them joint authority over Andorra, with the count representing the secular power. The Count of Foix assumed responsibilities related to matters of justice, taxation, and defense. They appointed local representatives, known as veguers, to oversee the secular administration of Andorra on their behalf.

The co-princeship of the Count of Foix brought a secular influence to Andorra's governance. Their involvement ensured the representation of secular interests and the preservation of the count's authority in the region. The count's role extended beyond administrative functions, as they were responsible for maintaining order, protecting the territory, and enforcing the pareatges.

The Count of Foix's position as co-prince bestowed upon them certain privileges and rights within the co-principality. They participated in ceremonial events, such as the inauguration of the co-princes and the coronation of the elected heads of government, reinforcing their symbolic and social significance in Andorran society.

The Count of Foix's involvement in Andorra's governance had implications for the socio-economic landscape of the region. Their role in matters of taxation, trade, and defense impacted the economic activities and prosperity of Andorra. The count's authority and influence contributed to the stability and development of the co-principality.

Historically, the Count of Foix faced challenges to their authority and claims to Andorra's sovereignty. Disputes over succession and territorial conflicts with neighboring powers tested the count's position as co-prince. However, through diplomatic negotiations and strategic alliances, the Count of Foix managed to assert and maintain their role within the co-principality.

In conclusion, the Count of Foix played a vital role in the birth of the co-principality of Andorra. Their involvement as the secular co-prince laid the foundation for the unique dual governance system. The pareatges, the agreements between the Count of Foix and the Bishop of Urgell, defined the shared sovereignty and responsibilities of the co-princes. The count's involvement in Andorra's governance, administration, and ceremonial events shaped the socio-political landscape of the co-principality. Their position as co-prince ensured the representation of secular interests and contributed to the stability and development of Andorra. The Count of Foix's role in matters of justice, taxation, and defense had tangible effects on the socio-economic fabric of the region.

The Consolidation of Andorra's Political Structure

The consolidation of Andorra's political structure marked a significant phase in its history, solidifying the foundations of the co-principality and shaping its governance for centuries to come. This chapter explores the historical developments and key factors that contributed to the consolidation of Andorra's political structure.

Throughout the medieval period, Andorra experienced a process of political consolidation as the co-princes, the Count of Foix and the Bishop of Urgell, worked to establish and maintain their joint authority. This consolidation was driven by various factors, including diplomatic negotiations, legal agreements, and the active participation of the Andorran people.

One important aspect of the consolidation process was the reaffirmation and renewal of the pareatges, the agreements between the co-princes. These pareatges served as the foundation of the co-principality, outlining the rights, responsibilities, and privileges of the co-princes and the Andorran population. Periodic renegotiations and reconfirmations of the pareatges ensured the continuity and stability of Andorra's political structure.

The consolidation of Andorra's political structure also relied on the active engagement and cooperation of the Andorran people, known as the paréage. The paréage played a crucial role in the governance and administration of the co-principality. Their participation in decision-making processes, the management of local affairs, and the provision of military service to the co-princes fostered a sense of shared responsibility and strengthened the political structure of Andorra.

The establishment of local institutions, such as the General Council, further contributed to the consolidation of Andorra's political structure. The General Council, composed of representatives from each parish, served as a platform for collective decision-making and the expression of the Andorran people's interests. The council played a vital role in the legislative process, ensuring that the voice of the paréage was heard in the governance of the co-principality.

The consolidation of Andorra's political structure was also influenced by external factors. The geopolitical context of the Pyrenees region, with its shifting power dynamics and the ambitions of neighboring powers, presented challenges to the co-princes and the stability of the co-principality. The ability of the co-princes to navigate these external pressures, maintain diplomatic relations, and preserve Andorra's autonomy contributed to the consolidation of its political structure.

Over time, Andorra's political structure continued to evolve and adapt to changing historical circumstances. The consolidation process involved not only the co-princes and the paréage but also the broader Andorran society. The political identity and collective memory of the Andorran people became intertwined with the co-principality, solidifying its political structure as a unique and cherished aspect of their cultural heritage.

The consolidation of Andorra's political structure had implications for the co-princes themselves. The Count of Foix and the Bishop of Urgell, while sharing sovereignty over Andorra, had to navigate their own interests and the broader regional politics. Their ability to maintain a delicate balance of power and preserve the co-principality's governance system contributed to its consolidation.

In conclusion, the consolidation of Andorra's political structure was a complex and dynamic process that involved diplomatic negotiations, legal agreements, the active participation of the Andorran people, and the navigation of external pressures. The reaffirmation of the pareatges, the establishment of local institutions, and the continued cooperation between the co-princes and the paréage contributed to the stability and continuity of Andorra's political structure. This consolidation laid the groundwork for the unique governance system that continues to shape Andorra's political landscape.

Feudalism and Land Tenure in Medieval Andorra

Feudalism and land tenure played pivotal roles in shaping the social, economic, and political landscape of medieval Andorra. This chapter explores the intricate dynamics of feudalism and the system of land ownership and control that prevailed in the co-principality during this era.

Feudalism, a hierarchical system based on the exchange of land for service and loyalty, was a fundamental aspect of medieval society. In Andorra, feudalism provided the framework for the distribution and management of land and the relationships between the different social classes.

At the top of the feudal hierarchy were the co-princes, the Bishop of Urgell and the Count of Foix, who held ultimate authority over the land. They were the primary landholders and granted parcels of land, known as fiefs, to their vassals in exchange for military service, economic contributions, and other obligations.

The vassals, who were typically nobles or knights, held their fiefs directly from the co-princes. They swore an oath of fealty and provided military service and other forms of support to the co-princes in return for their landholdings. The vassals were responsible for governing their territories, collecting taxes, maintaining law and order, and providing military assistance when called upon.

The distribution of land in Andorra was not solely limited to the noble class. Below the vassals were the peasants or serfs, who were the primary agricultural laborers and tenant farmers. The peasants worked the land and were subject to the authority of the local nobility. In exchange for their labor, they received protection and the right to work and live on the land.

Land tenure in medieval Andorra was often characterized by a mix of ownership and various forms of tenancy. The co-princes and nobles held outright ownership of the land, while others, such as the peasants, held it through various forms of leasehold or hereditary tenancy. The specific arrangements varied depending on the social status of the landholders and the terms set by the co-princes.

The system of land tenure in Andorra was closely tied to the feudal obligations and relationships between the landholders. The vassals owed military service, financial contributions, and other duties to the co-princes, while the peasants provided labor, produce, or other forms of tribute to their noble lords. These obligations were essential for maintaining the stability, defense, and economic functioning of the co-principality.

The land tenure system in Andorra also facilitated social stratification. The co-princes and nobles enjoyed significant privileges and held the highest positions of power and wealth. The vassals, though lower in rank, held substantial authority over their territories and had control over the labor and resources of the peasants. The peasants, as the lowest class, had limited social mobility and were bound to their land and the obligations imposed by their lords.

The feudal system of land tenure in Andorra was not without its complexities and tensions. Disputes over land ownership, inheritance, and the rights and obligations of the different classes occasionally arose. The resolution of these disputes often required the intervention of the co-princes, local authorities, or the ecclesiastical courts.

Over time, changes in the political and social landscape influenced the feudal system and land tenure in Andorra. External pressures, shifts in power dynamics, and evolving economic conditions affected the relationships between the co-princes, the nobles, and the peasants. However, the feudal system and the principles of land ownership and control remained central to the socio-economic structure of medieval Andorra.

In conclusion, feudalism and the system of land tenure were foundational elements of medieval Andorra. The co-princes and nobles held ownership and control over the land, distributing parcels to vassals in exchange for service and loyalty. The vassals, in turn, governed their territories, collected taxes, and provided military support to the co-princes. The peasants, as the laboring class, worked the land and owed obligations to the noble lords in exchange for protection and the right to occupy the land.

Andorra in the Reconquista: A Buffer Zone between Christians and Muslims

Andorra, located in the heart of the Pyrenees Mountains, played a unique role as a buffer zone between the Christian and Muslim realms during the period of the Reconquista. This chapter explores the historical context, the geopolitical significance of Andorra, and its position as a territorial boundary between Christians and Muslims.

The Reconquista refers to the centuries-long struggle by Christian kingdoms in the Iberian Peninsula to reclaim territories that had been occupied by Muslim forces. Andorra, situated in close proximity to the contested borderlands between the Christian kingdoms and the Muslim-ruled territories, found itself caught in the midst of this conflict.

During the early medieval period, the Muslim Moors had expanded their control into the Iberian Peninsula, establishing the Umayyad Caliphate of Al-Andalus. As Christian kingdoms began to mount campaigns to regain their lost territories, Andorra's strategic location made it an important area of contention.

Andorra's position in the Pyrenees Mountains made it a natural barrier between the Muslim-ruled territories to the south and the Christian kingdoms to the north. Its mountainous terrain, characterized by rugged landscapes and narrow passes, provided defensive advantages and made it challenging for large military forces to traverse.

As a result, Andorra became a significant buffer zone, serving as a territorial boundary that separated the expanding Christian kingdoms, such as Aragon and Catalonia, from the Muslim-ruled territories of Al-Andalus. The co-principality of Andorra emerged within this context as a space that allowed for a degree of autonomy while acting as a neutral ground between these competing forces.

The buffer zone status of Andorra allowed the co-princes, the Count of Foix and the Bishop of Urgell, to navigate the complex dynamics of the Reconquista. They could maintain relationships with both the Christian and Muslim powers while preserving the co-principality's independence and avoiding direct entanglement in the conflicts.

Andorra's neutrality and strategic position also made it an attractive location for diplomatic negotiations and trade. The co-princes could act as intermediaries between the Christian and Muslim realms, facilitating communication and potentially mitigating conflicts. Additionally, the merchants and travelers passing through Andorra benefited from the security provided by its buffer zone status.

While Andorra served as a buffer zone, it was not entirely immune to the influence and pressures of the Reconquista. The expansionist ambitions of both Christian and Muslim powers occasionally encroached upon Andorran territory, leading to territorial disputes and shifting allegiances. However, Andorra's geographical features and the delicate balance of power within the co-principality allowed for a relative degree of stability and autonomy.

The buffer zone status of Andorra gradually diminished as the Christian kingdoms made significant advancements in the Reconquista. With the gradual recapture of territories from the Moors, the immediate threats and pressures on Andorra's borders diminished. As a result, Andorra's role as a buffer zone evolved, and its focus shifted towards maintaining its autonomy and navigating its relationships with the surrounding powers.

In conclusion, Andorra's position as a buffer zone between Christians and Muslims during the Reconquista was a defining characteristic of its historical role. The co-principality's strategic location allowed it to act as a territorial boundary and maintain a certain degree of autonomy while facilitating diplomacy and trade. Although Andorra was not completely insulated from the pressures of the Reconquista, its buffer zone status allowed for a relatively stable and neutral existence within the broader context of the Christian-Muslim conflicts of the time.

Challenging Times: Andorra in the Hundred Years' War

The Hundred Years' War, a series of conflicts between the Kingdoms of England and France from the 14th to the 15th century, had a significant impact on the geopolitical situation in Europe. Andorra, nestled in the Pyrenees Mountains, found itself caught in the midst of this prolonged conflict. This chapter explores the challenges Andorra faced during the Hundred Years' War and its attempts to navigate the complex dynamics of the warring powers.

Andorra, as a co-principality, maintained its neutrality during the Hundred Years' War. Its strategic location in the Pyrenees Mountains, far from the main theaters of war, provided a degree of protection from direct military engagements. However, Andorra was not completely insulated from the repercussions and pressures arising from the conflict.

The Hundred Years' War had a profound impact on the neighboring regions of Aragon, Catalonia, and Occitania, which were directly involved in the conflict. As a result, Andorra's co-princes, the Count of Foix and the Bishop of Urgell, had to navigate the shifting alliances, territorial disputes, and power struggles that characterized the war-torn landscape of the surrounding regions.

The war created challenges for Andorra in several ways. Firstly, the proximity of Andorra to the conflict zones exposed it to potential incursions and raids by marauding bands, mercenaries, and desperate soldiers. These incursions threatened the security and well-being of the Andorran population, necessitating the strengthening of local defenses and the establishment of alliances for mutual protection.

Secondly, the economic consequences of the war impacted Andorra's trade and commerce. As the neighboring regions suffered from the ravages of war, trade routes were disrupted, and economic activities declined. Andorra, reliant on trade and its role as a crossroads, faced the challenge of maintaining economic stability and ensuring the livelihoods of its inhabitants.

Additionally, the Hundred Years' War had political implications for the co-princes and the governance of Andorra. The Count of Foix and the Bishop of Urgell had familial ties and allegiances that extended to the warring powers. The changing fortunes and shifting alliances of England and France influenced the diplomatic relationships of the co-princes, requiring them to carefully navigate their positions to preserve the co-principality's autonomy.

Diplomatic negotiations and alliances played a crucial role in Andorra's attempts to safeguard its interests during the war. The co-princes sought to maintain relationships with both England and France, ensuring that Andorra's neutrality was respected and that the co-principality could continue to thrive amidst the conflict. This delicate balancing act required diplomatic finesse and the ability to adapt to the ever-changing political landscape.

The Hundred Years' War had a lasting impact on Andorra, shaping its political, economic, and social trajectory. The war's conclusion in 1453 brought relative stability to the region, but it also left behind a legacy of political and cultural transformations. The repercussions of the war reverberated through subsequent centuries, influencing the geopolitical relationships and alliances that Andorra would forge.

In conclusion, the Hundred Years' War presented numerous challenges for Andorra, despite its neutral stance. The co-princes and the Andorran population had to navigate the threat of incursions, economic disruptions, and the complexities of diplomatic relationships. Andorra's ability to maintain its autonomy and adapt to the shifting dynamics of the war contributed to its resilience in the face of challenging times. The repercussions of the war would leave a lasting impact on Andorra's political, economic, and social landscape, shaping its trajectory in the centuries to come.

Border Disputes and the Impact on Andorra's Sovereignty

Border disputes have played a significant role in shaping Andorra's history and have had a direct impact on its sovereignty. This chapter delves into the complexities of border disputes involving Andorra, examining their historical context, the parties involved, and the consequences for Andorra's sovereignty.

Andorra's unique geographical location, nestled in the Pyrenees Mountains, has made it susceptible to border conflicts and disputes throughout history. The co-principality's position as a territorial boundary between various powers has made it subject to competing territorial claims and disputes over land.

One of the earliest border disputes involving Andorra can be traced back to the medieval period when neighboring feudal lords vied for control over the region. The Count of Foix and the Bishop of Urgell, as co-princes, had to navigate these disputes and assert their authority over Andorra's territory. The conflicts often revolved around defining the precise boundaries and determining the extent of their respective jurisdictions.

The external powers that surrounded Andorra, such as France and Spain, also contributed to border disputes. These larger powers, seeking to consolidate their territories and assert their dominance, occasionally challenged the boundaries of Andorra. The shifting political alliances and conflicts between these powers further complicated the border disputes and created an environment of uncertainty for the co-principality.

One notable border dispute in Andorra's history involved France and Spain. During the 18th and 19th centuries, these two powers engaged in a protracted disagreement over the demarcation of their respective borders with Andorra. The dispute centered on determining which power had legitimate control over certain areas surrounding Andorra.

The consequences of border disputes for Andorra's sovereignty were significant. They posed a direct challenge to the co-princes' authority and threatened the co-principality's autonomy. The resolution of these disputes required diplomatic negotiations, legal agreements, and the involvement of external mediators or arbiters.

In some cases, border disputes led to territorial adjustments that altered the boundaries of Andorra. Agreements, such as treaties or conventions, were reached to define and clarify the borders, often with the involvement of the co-princes and the neighboring powers. These border delineations sought to safeguard Andorra's territorial integrity and reaffirm its sovereignty.

The resolution of border disputes has not always been straightforward, and their impact on Andorra's sovereignty has varied over time. Some disputes were resolved through diplomatic means, while others required legal processes or the intervention of external authorities. The resolution of these conflicts often necessitated compromises and concessions from all parties involved.

It is important to note that the specifics of border disputes involving Andorra may vary depending on the historical period and the parties involved. The historical records provide insights into the general trends and patterns of border conflicts, but the intricate details of individual disputes may not be fully documented.

In conclusion, border disputes have had a profound impact on Andorra's sovereignty throughout its history. The co-principality's position as a territorial boundary and the involvement of neighboring powers in asserting their claims have led to conflicts over land and challenges to the co-princes' authority. The resolution of these disputes has required diplomatic negotiations, legal agreements, and compromises to preserve Andorra's territorial integrity and reaffirm its sovereignty. The border disputes serve as a testament to the complex nature of Andorra's geopolitical landscape and the ongoing efforts to maintain its autonomy within a changing political environment.

The Influence of the Catholic Church in Medieval Andorra

The Catholic Church held significant influence in medieval Andorra, shaping various aspects of religious, social, and political life. This chapter explores the extent of the Catholic Church's influence in Andorra during this period, highlighting its role in religious practices, governance, and the development of cultural norms.

The Catholic Church, as an institution, played a central role in the spiritual life of medieval Andorra. It provided religious guidance, administered sacraments, and upheld moral and ethical standards within the co-principality. The Church's teachings and rituals formed the foundation of religious practices and shaped the beliefs and values of the Andorran population.

The Bishop of Urgell, as one of the co-princes of Andorra, held ecclesiastical authority and was responsible for overseeing the religious affairs of the co-principality. The bishop's influence extended beyond religious matters and encompassed aspects of governance, education, and the administration of justice. Their role as a spiritual leader and co-prince brought together both secular and religious authority.

The Catholic Church's influence in Andorra was evident in the presence of religious institutions and the construction of churches, monasteries, and chapels. These religious structures served as places of worship, centers of community life, and repositories of religious artifacts and artworks. They also functioned as symbols of the

Church's influence and provided a sense of spiritual cohesion within the co-principality.

The Church's influence also extended to education and the dissemination of knowledge. Monastic orders, such as the Benedictines, played a crucial role in the preservation and transmission of knowledge through their scriptoria and libraries. They were centers of learning, where manuscripts were copied, illuminated, and preserved. The Church's emphasis on education contributed to the intellectual and cultural development of medieval Andorra.

The Catholic Church had a significant impact on the legal and judicial systems in Andorra. Ecclesiastical courts, overseen by the Bishop of Urgell, were responsible for administering justice in matters related to canon law. These courts handled cases involving marriage, inheritance, and moral transgressions, among other issues. The Church's involvement in the legal sphere ensured the application of religious principles and the maintenance of moral order within the co-principality.

The Church's influence in Andorra was also manifested in the development of cultural norms and practices. Religious festivals, processions, and rituals formed an integral part of Andorran society. These religious celebrations, such as the Feast of Saint John the Baptist and the Feast of Our Lady of Meritxell, provided opportunities for communal gatherings, expressions of faith, and the reinforcement of religious identity.

Charitable activities were another important aspect of the Church's influence in Andorra. Religious orders and individuals engaged in acts of charity, such as providing assistance to the poor, caring for the sick, and supporting the less fortunate. These acts of compassion were rooted in the Christian teachings of love, compassion, and social responsibility.

It is important to acknowledge that the influence of the Catholic Church in Andorra was not uniform throughout the medieval period. The exact extent and nature of its influence varied depending on factors such as the specific time period, the individuals involved, and the broader historical context.

In conclusion, the Catholic Church exerted significant influence in medieval Andorra, shaping religious practices, governance, education, legal systems, and cultural norms. The Church's teachings and rituals provided a moral and spiritual framework for the Andorran population. The ecclesiastical authority of the Bishop of Urgell extended beyond religious matters, encompassing aspects of governance and justice. The Church's presence in Andorra through religious institutions, educational centers, and charitable activities contributed to the cohesion and development of the co-principality.

Trade and Commerce in Medieval Andorra

Trade and commerce played a vital role in the economic development and cultural exchange of medieval Andorra. This chapter explores the dynamics of trade, the routes and networks involved, the goods traded, and the impact of commercial activities on Andorran society.

Despite its mountainous terrain, Andorra was not isolated from the larger economic networks of the medieval world. Situated along major trade routes that connected the Iberian Peninsula with the rest of Europe, Andorra served as a crucial crossroads for merchants and travelers. Its strategic location in the Pyrenees Mountains allowed it to benefit from the flow of goods and ideas between different regions.

The main trade routes passing through Andorra connected the Mediterranean coast with northern Europe. Merchants traveling from the Mediterranean ports, such as Barcelona or Tarragona, traversed the mountain passes of Andorra to reach the markets of France and beyond. These routes facilitated the exchange of goods and fostered economic interactions between various regions.

The types of goods traded in medieval Andorra were diverse, reflecting the needs and desires of the population. Agricultural products, such as grains, livestock, and wine, formed the backbone of the local economy. Andorra's fertile valleys and suitable climate allowed for the cultivation of crops and the rearing of livestock. These agricultural products were traded locally and also served as commodities for regional and international trade.

Apart from agricultural goods, Andorra's strategic location made it a hub for the exchange of other commodities. Raw materials, such as timber, minerals, and stone, were traded, taking advantage of the region's natural resources. Craftsmanship and artisanal goods, including textiles, leather goods, and metalwork, also contributed to the trade and commerce of the co-principality.

The markets of Andorra thrived as merchants from different regions converged to engage in commercial activities. Fairs and marketplaces, such as the Escaldes-Engordany Fair and the Sant Julià de Lòria Market, provided opportunities for trade and economic exchange. These gatherings facilitated the exchange of goods, the formation of business relationships, and the promotion of cultural exchange.

The economic prosperity of Andorra was further supported by the presence of local artisans, who played a crucial role in producing goods for trade. Skilled craftsmen, such as blacksmiths, potters, weavers, and carpenters, contributed to the diversity of products available in the markets. Their craftsmanship and specialization added value to the local economy and enhanced the reputation of Andorran goods.

The economic activities in medieval Andorra were not limited to local trade alone. The co-principality also participated in long-distance trade networks, linking it to distant regions. Merchants from Andorra engaged in trade with major centers such as Barcelona, Toulouse, Lyon, and even cities as far as Venice and Genoa. These long-distance trade connections expanded the range of goods available in Andorra and contributed to its economic growth.

The prosperity of trade in medieval Andorra had broader societal implications. It stimulated the growth of towns and villages, as well as the development of infrastructure such as roads and bridges to facilitate trade. The accumulation of wealth through trade enabled the emergence of a merchant class, contributing to social mobility and the diversification of Andorran society.

The influence of trade extended beyond the economic sphere. Cultural exchange, as a result of commercial interactions, enriched the co-principality. Merchants brought new ideas, technologies, and cultural practices from different regions, contributing to the intellectual and cultural development of Andorra.

In conclusion, trade and commerce played a pivotal role in the economic prosperity and cultural exchange of medieval Andorra. The strategic location of the co-principality along major trade routes facilitated the flow of goods and ideas. Agricultural products, raw materials, and artisanal goods formed the basis of trade in Andorra, with local and long-distance networks connecting the co-principality to various regions. The presence of markets, fairs, and skilled artisans fostered economic interactions and contributed to the growth of Andorra's towns and villages.

The Catalan-Aragonese Union and Andorra

The Catalan-Aragonese Union, a political alliance between the Crown of Aragon and the Principality of Catalonia, had a significant impact on the history of Andorra. This chapter explores the origins of the union, its implications for Andorra, and the enduring influence it had on the co-principality.

The Catalan-Aragonese Union came into effect in 1137 through the marriage of Ramon Berenguer IV, Count of Barcelona, and Petronilla of Aragon, heiress to the Kingdom of Aragon. This dynastic union brought together the territories of Catalonia and Aragon under a single ruling house, establishing a closer political relationship between the two regions.

Andorra, situated within the borders of Catalonia, became directly affected by the Catalan-Aragonese Union. The co-princes of Andorra, the Count of Foix and the Bishop of Urgell, held significant titles within the Catalan-Aragonese realm, further strengthening the ties between Andorra and the union.

The union had far-reaching consequences for Andorra's governance and political landscape. It solidified the authority of the co-princes and their connection to the wider Catalan-Aragonese domains. The Count of Foix, as a vassal of the King of Aragon, held the title of Viscount of Béarn and was a prominent noble within the union. The Bishop of Urgell, on the other hand, held ecclesiastical authority and represented the Church's interests in the union.

The Catalan-Aragonese Union brought administrative and legal reforms to Andorra. It introduced the legal framework of Catalan law, known as the Usages of Catalonia, which influenced the co-principality's legal system. The Usages provided a standardized set of laws and regulations that governed various aspects of Andorran society, including land tenure, inheritance, and judicial procedures.

Furthermore, the union's influence extended to the cultural and linguistic aspects of Andorran society. The Catalan language became the dominant linguistic and cultural influence, shaping the language spoken and written in Andorra. Catalan customs, traditions, and cultural practices became deeply ingrained in the co-principality, contributing to the cultural identity of Andorra.

The Catalan-Aragonese Union also played a role in shaping Andorra's external relations. The union expanded its influence beyond the Iberian Peninsula, with the Crown of Aragon establishing a maritime empire that encompassed territories in the Mediterranean, including Sardinia, Sicily, and Naples. Andorra, though a landlocked co-principality, benefited from the union's connections and trade networks, further enhancing its economic prospects.

The union faced challenges and complexities over time. Succession disputes, political conflicts, and changing alliances occasionally strained the relationship between Catalonia and Aragon. These tensions were reflected in

Andorra, with periodic disagreements and power struggles between the co-princes and their respective domains. However, the union persisted, maintaining its influence over Andorra's political and cultural spheres.

The Catalan-Aragonese Union endured for centuries, shaping Andorra's historical trajectory until the 18th century. The union eventually dissolved with the succession crisis in the late 17th century and the War of Spanish Succession in the early 18th century. The aftermath of these events led to changes in Andorra's political relationships, as the co-princes' authority became more closely aligned with external powers.

In conclusion, the Catalan-Aragonese Union played a pivotal role in the history of Andorra. The union solidified the ties between Catalonia and Aragon, directly influencing the co-principality's governance, legal system, cultural identity, and external relations. The co-princes, with their titles and connections within the union, held significant influence over Andorra and shaped its development. The administrative and legal reforms introduced through the union established a standardized framework for Andorra's governance, ensuring consistency and stability.

Andorra and the Kingdom of France: The Treaty of Corbeil

The Treaty of Corbeil, signed in 1258, marked a significant turning point in the relationship between Andorra and the Kingdom of France. This chapter delves into the historical context, negotiations, and implications of the treaty, shedding light on the dynamics between Andorra and France during this period.

In the 13th century, Andorra found itself situated in a region of shifting political alliances and territorial claims. France, under the rule of King Louis IX, sought to consolidate its control over the territories in the Pyrenees. Andorra, as a landlocked co-principality, was strategically positioned in the borderlands between France and the emerging Kingdom of Aragon.

The Treaty of Corbeil was the result of negotiations between Roger-Bernard III, Count of Foix and co-prince of Andorra, and King Louis IX of France. The treaty solidified the political relationship between Andorra and France, defining the rights and responsibilities of both parties. It acknowledged the co-princes' authority over Andorra while recognizing French suzerainty.

Under the terms of the treaty, Andorra was granted certain rights and privileges, including the preservation of its internal governance and the right to self-administration. The co-princes, as vassals of the French Crown, were entrusted with the task of maintaining order, collecting taxes, and ensuring the loyalty of the Andorran population.

The Treaty of Corbeil also outlined France's role in Andorra's external affairs. The co-princes agreed to defend Andorra against external threats, and Andorra pledged allegiance to the French Crown. This recognition of French suzerainty established a framework for Andorra's relationship with France, emphasizing the co-principality's position as a buffer zone and strategic outpost along the French border.

The treaty had implications for Andorra's territorial boundaries as well. It clarified that Andorra would not be subject to any territorial claims or encroachments from the neighboring regions of Catalonia or Aragon. This provision aimed to safeguard Andorra's autonomy and prevent disputes over its territorial integrity.

Furthermore, the Treaty of Corbeil highlighted the economic and trade aspects of Andorra's relationship with France. It granted Andorra certain privileges, including exemptions from certain tolls and customs duties when conducting trade with France. This facilitated the flow of goods and fostered economic exchanges between Andorra and its powerful neighbor.

The treaty's influence on Andorra's internal affairs was substantial. It recognized the co-princes' authority and their right to govern Andorra according to their own laws and customs. The co-princes, in turn, pledged their allegiance to the French Crown and agreed to respect the interests of France within the co-principality.

Over the centuries, the Treaty of Corbeil remained in effect, shaping the relationship between Andorra and France. It provided a framework for cooperation, ensuring that Andorra maintained its autonomy while acknowledging French suzerainty. The treaty allowed Andorra to navigate the complex geopolitical landscape of the region and maintain a certain degree of independence.

It is important to note that while the Treaty of Corbeil established the foundation of the relationship between Andorra and France, subsequent agreements and historical events would shape the evolving dynamics between the two entities. The treaty laid the groundwork for Andorra's status as a co-principality and its unique position within the geopolitical landscape.

In conclusion, the Treaty of Corbeil played a significant role in defining the relationship between Andorra and the Kingdom of France. It solidified the co-princes' authority, acknowledged French suzerainty, and provided a framework for the governance and external relations of the co-principality. The treaty's provisions ensured Andorra's autonomy, protected its territorial integrity, and facilitated economic exchanges with France. While subsequent agreements and historical developments would shape the relationship further, the Treaty of Corbeil marked an important milestone in the history of Andorra's interactions with the Kingdom of France.

The War of the Spanish Succession and its Effect on Andorra

The War of the Spanish Succession, which raged from 1701 to 1714, had a profound impact on Andorra, as it became embroiled in the wider conflict for control over the Spanish throne. This chapter explores the historical context, key events, and consequences of the war on Andorra, highlighting the political, social, and economic effects.

The War of the Spanish Succession erupted following the death of the Spanish king, Charles II, in 1700. The lack of a clear heir to the Spanish throne led to competing claims and a struggle for dominance among European powers. The war pitted the Bourbon dynasty, represented by Philip V of Spain, against the Habsburg claimant, Archduke Charles of Austria.

Andorra, as a co-principality, found itself caught in the crossfire of this conflict. The co-princes of Andorra, who held their titles from the Bishop of Urgell and the Count of Foix (later replaced by the King of France), had to navigate a delicate balance between their allegiances to the opposing factions. The Bishop of Urgell, traditionally aligned with the Habsburgs, supported Archduke Charles, while the French-backed Count of Foix pledged loyalty to Philip V.

The involvement of Andorra in the war was not limited to mere political alignments. The co-principality became a battleground for the rival factions, with military actions and skirmishes taking place within its borders. Andorra's strategic location in the Pyrenees Mountains made it a crucial passageway for troops and supplies, further intensifying its entanglement in the conflict.

The consequences of the war on Andorra were multifaceted. The co-princes, as representatives of the rival factions, faced challenges in maintaining control and authority within the co-principality. The loyalty of the Andorran population was divided, with individuals aligning themselves with either the Habsburg or Bourbon cause. This internal division created tensions and frictions within Andorran society.

The war also had a significant economic impact on Andorra. The disruption of trade routes, pillaging, and requisitioning of resources by the warring factions hindered the co-principality's economic activities. The population faced hardships, as the conflict brought about economic instability, scarcity of goods, and loss of livelihoods. Andorra's geographical position as a battleground further exacerbated the economic difficulties faced by its inhabitants.

Furthermore, the war had repercussions for Andorra's political relationships. The outcome of the war would determine the fate of the Spanish throne and, consequently, the co-princes' allegiance. As the conflict progressed, it became apparent that Philip V of Spain, supported by France, would emerge victorious. This shift in power dynamics led to a closer alignment of the co-princes with the Bourbon cause, as they sought to secure their positions and protect Andorra's autonomy.

The war finally came to an end in 1714 with the signing of the Treaty of Utrecht. The treaty recognized Philip V as the legitimate King of Spain but imposed certain conditions and limitations on his rule. Andorra's status as a co-principality was reaffirmed, and the co-princes' authority was preserved. However, the war had left its mark on Andorra, reshaping its political, social, and economic landscape.

In the aftermath of the war, Andorra had to rebuild and recover from the devastation inflicted during the conflict. The co-princes, now firmly aligned with the Bourbon cause, faced the task of restoring order, stabilizing the economy, and rebuilding the co-principality. Efforts were made to revitalize trade and commerce, repair infrastructure, and alleviate the hardships faced by the population.

The Age of Enlightenment and Andorra's Intellectual Awakening

The Age of Enlightenment, spanning from the late 17th to the 18th century, was a period of intellectual and cultural transformation across Europe. Andorra, though a small co-principality nestled in the Pyrenees Mountains, experienced its own intellectual awakening during this era. This chapter explores the influences, key figures, and intellectual developments that shaped Andorra's engagement with the ideas of the Enlightenment.

The Enlightenment was characterized by a shift towards reason, critical thinking, and the pursuit of knowledge. It emphasized the importance of individual rights, liberty, and the power of human intellect to improve society. While Andorra's geographical isolation may have limited direct exposure to the intellectual centers of Europe, the ideas of the Enlightenment gradually reached the co-principality through various channels.

One significant influence on Andorra's intellectual awakening during the Enlightenment was the broader cultural exchange facilitated by the co-princes' connections with neighboring regions. The Count of Foix, and later the King of France, maintained relationships with intellectual circles in France and beyond. This allowed for the dissemination of Enlightenment ideas into Andorran society.

The educational institutions of Andorra played a crucial role in fostering the intellectual awakening of the time. The establishment of schools and the growth of education in the co-principality provided a platform for the spread of Enlightenment thought. Students and teachers who had exposure to Enlightenment ideas in other regions brought their knowledge and perspectives back to Andorra, contributing to a growing intellectual climate.

The emergence of literary societies and intellectual salons further facilitated the exchange of ideas in Andorra. These gatherings, often organized by educated individuals, provided a platform for intellectual discourse, debates, and the dissemination of new philosophical and scientific concepts. Intellectuals and thinkers within Andorran society found a space to engage with the ideas of the Enlightenment and challenge prevailing notions.

One notable figure in Andorra's intellectual awakening was Antoni Fiter i Rossell, an Andorran priest and scholar who lived during the 18th century. Fiter i Rossell was a prolific writer and thinker who engaged with the ideas of the Enlightenment, particularly in the fields of history, natural sciences, and philosophy. His works, such as "Orígens i Successos de la Vila i Parròquia d'Andorra" and "Els Cosmògrafs Andorrans," reflected his engagement with Enlightenment thought and contributed to the intellectual discourse within the co-principality.

The Enlightenment also influenced the legal and political spheres of Andorra. The principles of reason, equality, and justice espoused during this period prompted discussions on the reform of legal systems and governance structures. While the specific reforms implemented in Andorra may have been limited, the intellectual currents of the Enlightenment had a catalyzing effect on the thinking around legal and political issues within the co-principality.

The impact of the Enlightenment on Andorra's society extended beyond intellectual circles. Enlightenment ideas gradually permeated various aspects of life, including religious beliefs, social practices, and cultural norms. The emphasis on reason and individualism challenged traditional religious dogmas and prompted critical thinking about social hierarchies and inequalities.

It is important to acknowledge that Andorra's engagement with the ideas of the Enlightenment was shaped by its unique historical and cultural context. The co-principality's small size, geographical isolation, and its political and religious structures influenced the pace and extent of its intellectual awakening. The influence of Enlightenment ideas may have been more limited compared to larger European centers, but it nonetheless left an indelible mark on Andorran intellectual and cultural life.

In conclusion, the Age of Enlightenment had a transformative effect on Andorra's intellectual landscape. Through cultural exchange, educational institutions, literary societies, and the contributions of notable figures such as Antoni Fiter i Rossell, Andorra experienced its own intellectual awakening during this era. The dissemination of Enlightenment ideas, though influenced by the co-principality's unique circumstances, fostered a spirit of critical thinking, scientific inquiry, and the questioning of traditional beliefs.

Andorra's Resilience: Surviving the Napoleonic Era

The Napoleonic Era, spanning from the late 18th to the early 19th century, brought significant upheaval and transformative changes to Europe. Andorra, though a small co-principality nestled in the Pyrenees Mountains, faced its own challenges during this tumultuous period. This chapter explores Andorra's resilience in the face of Napoleonic influences, highlighting the co-principality's ability to navigate the complexities of the era and preserve its unique identity.

The Napoleonic Era was characterized by the rise and consolidation of Napoleon Bonaparte's power in France, his expansionist policies, and the ensuing conflicts across Europe. Andorra's geographical location, situated between France and Spain, placed it within the sphere of Napoleon's ambitions and the repercussions of his actions.

As Napoleon's forces swept through Europe, they sought to establish political control and impose reforms aligned with the ideals of the French Revolution. Andorra, with its centuries-old co-principality governed by the Bishop of Urgell and the French co-prince, faced the challenge of reconciling its existing political structures with the demands and pressures of the Napoleonic regime.

During the early stages of the Napoleonic Era, Andorra managed to maintain a degree of autonomy and resist direct French interference. The co-princes upheld their authority and sought to protect Andorra's interests within the constraints of the changing political landscape. However, as Napoleon's influence grew, Andorra found itself caught between the ambitions of the French Empire and the interests of neighboring powers.

In 1806, Napoleon issued a decree that formally incorporated Andorra into the French Empire. This act signaled a significant shift in Andorra's political status and raised concerns about the co-principality's survival. The French administration sought to introduce centralized governance and implement reforms consistent with French laws and institutions.

Despite these challenges, Andorra displayed remarkable resilience during the Napoleonic Era. The co-princes, in collaboration with local authorities and the Andorran population, navigated the complex political environment and worked to safeguard the co-principality's distinct identity and traditions. They sought to negotiate favorable terms with the French administration and protect Andorra's unique status within the broader context of the Napoleonic Empire.

The resilience of Andorra was also evident in the preservation of its legal and administrative systems. While some elements of French law and governance were introduced, the co-principality managed to maintain its own legal traditions and internal structures. The Usages of Catalonia, the customary law that had long governed Andorra, continued to hold sway, providing a sense of continuity and familiarity for the Andorran population.

Additionally, Andorra's geographical position played a role in its survival during the Napoleonic Era. The mountainous terrain and rugged landscape made it a challenging territory to conquer and control. This natural barrier provided a measure of protection and allowed Andorra to maintain a degree of autonomy and independence.

The end of the Napoleonic Era brought about significant changes in Europe. Napoleon's downfall and the subsequent Congress of Vienna in 1815 reshaped the political map of the continent. Andorra's status and political relationships were once again subject to negotiation and realignment.

In the aftermath of the Napoleonic Era, Andorra regained its independence and resumed its position as a co-principality governed by the Bishop of Urgell and the French co-prince. The resilience demonstrated by Andorra throughout this challenging period ensured the preservation of its unique identity and political structure.

It is important to note that the impact of the Napoleonic Era on Andorra was not uniform. The specific details of Andorra's experiences during this time can be difficult to ascertain due to limited historical records. The co-princes and the Andorran population have left few written accounts of their experiences during the Napoleonic Era, making it challenging to provide a comprehensive narrative of the period.

However, it is clear that Andorra's resilience played a crucial role in its survival during this tumultuous era. The co-princes' ability to navigate the shifting political landscape, negotiate with external powers, and protect Andorra's autonomy were instrumental in safeguarding the co-principality's distinct identity.

Andorra's resilience was not limited to its political survival. The co-principality also managed to preserve its cultural heritage and traditions amidst the changes sweeping across Europe. The Andorran population's attachment to their customs, language, and way of life helped fortify their resilience in the face of external pressures.

The resilience of Andorra was a testament to the resilience of its people. The Andorran population demonstrated adaptability and resourcefulness, finding ways to cope with the challenges posed by the Napoleonic Era. The solidarity and cohesion within the co-principality played a crucial role in its ability to weather the storm and maintain its unique character.

It is worth noting that the Napoleonic Era had a lasting impact on Andorra's political and social landscape. The changes introduced during this period, even if temporary, left their mark on the co-principality. The experiences of the Napoleonic Era would influence subsequent developments and shape Andorra's interactions with neighboring powers in the years to come.

In conclusion, Andorra's resilience during the Napoleonic Era allowed the co-principality to navigate the challenges posed by the changing political landscape. The co-princes' diplomatic efforts, the preservation of Andorra's legal and administrative systems, and the population's attachment to their cultural heritage all contributed to Andorra's survival and the preservation of its distinct identity. The experiences of the Napoleonic Era shaped Andorra's trajectory and highlighted the co-principality's ability to endure and adapt in the face of external pressures.

Andorra in the 20th Century: From Agrarian Society to Tourism Hub

The 20th century brought significant transformations to Andorra, propelling the co-principality from an agrarian society into a thriving tourism destination. This chapter explores the key developments, social changes, and economic shifts that shaped Andorra's trajectory during this period.

At the turn of the 20th century, Andorra remained a predominantly rural and agrarian society. Agriculture, including livestock farming and small-scale crop cultivation, was the primary economic activity. The population largely relied on subsistence farming and self-sufficiency to sustain their livelihoods.

The first half of the 20th century was marked by challenges and disruptions for Andorra. The outbreak of World War I in 1914 and the subsequent Spanish Civil War from 1936 to 1939 had indirect impacts on the co-principality. While Andorra itself did not participate in these conflicts, its geographical proximity to the warring nations and its economic connections with neighboring regions meant that the population faced hardships and economic difficulties.

The isolated nature of Andorra, tucked away in the Pyrenees Mountains, limited its exposure to wider geopolitical events. However, the co-principality did not remain untouched by the political and social shifts that characterized the 20th century. The rise of fascist regimes in Europe and the ideological divisions of the Cold War had reverberations within Andorran society, even if on a smaller scale.

The mid-20th century saw the beginnings of a shift towards a more diversified economy in Andorra. The co-principality gradually embraced tourism as a means of economic development. The pristine natural beauty of the Pyrenees Mountains, coupled with its favorable geographical location between France and Spain, positioned Andorra as an attractive destination for outdoor activities, skiing, and mountain tourism.

The development of tourism in Andorra was supported by infrastructure improvements and the expansion of services to accommodate visitors. Hotels, resorts, and recreational facilities were established to cater to the growing number of tourists. Additionally, the accessibility of Andorra improved with the construction of roads and transportation networks, facilitating travel to and within the co-principality.

The growth of tourism brought about significant socio-economic changes in Andorra. The influx of visitors created employment opportunities beyond traditional agricultural activities. The service sector expanded, providing jobs in hospitality, retail, and other tourism-related industries. This shift in the labor market led to increased urbanization and population growth in urban areas, particularly in the capital, Andorra la Vella.

Furthermore, the economic transformation propelled Andorra's integration into the global economy. The co-principality fostered international partnerships and trade agreements, attracting foreign investment and fostering economic diversification. This shift from an agrarian society to a tourism-oriented economy allowed Andorra to generate revenue, improve infrastructure, and raise the standard of living for its population.

Despite the economic progress, Andorra remained committed to preserving its cultural heritage and identity. Efforts were made to maintain a balance between economic development and the protection of the co-principality's natural environment. Environmental regulations and sustainable practices were implemented to ensure the long-term preservation of the mountainous landscapes that drew visitors to Andorra.

The late 20th century witnessed further advancements in Andorra's tourism sector. The co-principality continued to attract visitors from around the world, particularly during the winter months for skiing and other winter sports. The growth of tourism not only bolstered the economy but also contributed to the diversification of Andorra's cultural landscape as it welcomed people from different backgrounds and nationalities.

In recent decades, Andorra has continued to evolve as a tourism hub while also diversifying its economy further. The co-principality has embraced other sectors such as finance, technology, and trade, aiming to capitalize on its favorable tax policies and strategic location. The development of modern infrastructure, including the expansion of shopping centers, entertainment venues, and cultural institutions, has enhanced Andorra's appeal as a destination for leisure and business travelers alike.

Andorra's transition into a tourism hub has not been without its challenges. The co-principality has had to manage the delicate balance between catering to the needs of tourists and preserving its cultural heritage. Efforts have been made to promote sustainable tourism practices, protect natural resources, and maintain the authenticity of local traditions and customs. The co-princes and the Andorran government have implemented regulations and initiatives to ensure responsible tourism and minimize the environmental impact of increased visitor numbers.

The growth of tourism in Andorra has had a significant impact on the local population. The influx of visitors has created employment opportunities across various sectors, from hospitality and retail to outdoor activities and entertainment. The development of tourism infrastructure has also contributed to improvements in public services, transportation networks, and the overall quality of life for residents.

The shift towards a tourism-based economy has resulted in urbanization and the transformation of urban areas. Andorra la Vella, as the capital and commercial center, has experienced significant growth and development. Modern buildings, shopping districts, and cultural landmarks now characterize the cityscape, reflecting the changing economic landscape and the evolving needs of residents and visitors.

Andorra's success as a tourism hub can be attributed to a combination of factors. Its geographical location, nestled in the Pyrenees Mountains, provides a picturesque backdrop and offers diverse recreational opportunities, including skiing, hiking, and mountain biking. The co-principality's tax advantages and political stability have also attracted foreign investment and business ventures, contributing to its economic growth.

In recent years, Andorra has continued to innovate and adapt to changing tourism trends. The co-principality has embraced digitalization and online platforms to promote tourism, streamline visitor experiences, and facilitate online bookings. Efforts have been made to diversify the tourism offerings beyond winter sports, with investments in cultural events, music festivals, and wellness tourism.

It is important to note that the growth of tourism in Andorra has not been without its challenges. The co-principality must carefully manage visitor numbers to ensure the sustainability of its natural resources and the preservation of its unique identity. Balancing the demands of tourism with the needs of the local population remains an ongoing concern.

In conclusion, the 20th century witnessed a remarkable transformation for Andorra as it evolved from an agrarian society into a thriving tourism hub. The shift towards tourism brought about significant socio-economic changes, including urbanization, job creation, and economic diversification. Andorra's natural beauty, strategic location, and favorable tax policies have positioned it as an attractive destination for visitors from around the world. While embracing tourism, Andorra has also made efforts to preserve its cultural heritage and protect its environment, aiming to ensure a sustainable and authentic experience for visitors.

Contemporary Andorra: Economy, Society, and Governance

Contemporary Andorra is a co-principality that has undergone remarkable transformations in its economy, society, and governance. This chapter explores the key features and developments that characterize present-day Andorra, highlighting its economic diversification, social dynamics, and unique political structure.

Andorra's economy has evolved significantly in recent decades, moving beyond its traditional reliance on agriculture and tourism. The co-principality has strategically positioned itself as a financial and business center, attracting foreign investment and capitalizing on its favorable tax environment. The banking and finance sector, along with ancillary services such as wealth management and investment funds, has become a vital component of Andorra's economy. The country's banking secrecy laws, while subject to international scrutiny, have played a role in attracting businesses and individuals seeking financial services.

Alongside the financial sector, Andorra has diversified its economic base to include retail, trade, real estate, and technology. The development of commercial centers and shopping districts has fostered a vibrant retail sector, drawing shoppers from both residents and visitors. The co-principality's tax advantages, combined with its strategic location and modern infrastructure, have facilitated trade and commerce, contributing to economic growth.

Tourism continues to be an important sector in Andorra's economy. The co-principality attracts visitors throughout the year, offering diverse outdoor activities, ski resorts, spa retreats, and cultural events. Andorra's accessibility, with well-developed transportation networks and close proximity to major European cities, has contributed to its appeal as a tourist destination.

Andorra's population has grown steadily in recent years, with a diverse mix of residents from different nationalities and backgrounds. The majority of the population consists of Andorran nationals, but there is also a significant presence of foreign residents, including individuals attracted by employment opportunities, lifestyle factors, and the favorable tax environment. The multicultural nature of Andorran society has contributed to a vibrant social fabric, with diverse cultural influences and a cosmopolitan atmosphere.

The co-principality places a strong emphasis on education, with a well-developed education system that includes both public and private institutions. Education is compulsory for Andorran children between the ages of 6 and 16. The co-principality also invests in vocational training and higher education to meet the evolving needs of its economy and provide opportunities for professional development.

Andorra's healthcare system is characterized by a combination of public and private providers. The co-principality has made efforts to ensure accessible and quality healthcare services for its population, with a focus on preventive care and health promotion. The Andorran healthcare system benefits from collaborations with neighboring countries, particularly Spain and France, for specialized medical services.

Andorra's unique political structure is based on a co-principality, with the Bishop of Urgell and the President of France serving as co-princes. The co-princes' role is largely symbolic, and the day-to-day governance of the co-principality is carried out by a parliamentary system. Andorra has a parliamentary democracy, with a unicameral legislature known as the General Council. Members of the General Council are elected by universal suffrage and serve four-year terms.

The Andorran government, headed by the Head of Government, exercises executive power and is responsible for policy-making and administration. The government's activities span various sectors, including finance, economy, social welfare, and infrastructure development. Andorra has sought to promote transparency, accountability, and good governance practices, aligning its policies with international standards.

Andorra is not a member of the European Union (EU), but it maintains close relations with the EU through various agreements. The co-principality uses the euro as its official currency, and it participates in certain EU initiatives and programs. While Andorra is not part of the Schengen Area, it has implemented measures to facilitate travel and border management in collaboration with neighboring countries.

In recent years, Andorra has been proactive in enhancing its international relations and participating in global organizations. It has become a member of international bodies such as the United Nations (UN), the Organization for Security and Cooperation in Europe (OSCE), and the Council of Europe. These memberships reflect Andorra's commitment to engaging with the international community and contributing to global discussions on various issues.

Andorra places great importance on its environmental stewardship and sustainable development. The co-principality is known for its efforts to preserve its natural landscapes, protect biodiversity, and promote eco-friendly practices. Environmental regulations are in place to ensure responsible development and the conservation of Andorra's pristine mountainous environment.

Social welfare is a priority for the Andorran government, with programs in place to support vulnerable populations, provide healthcare services, and address social inequalities. The co-principality has a strong social security system that offers benefits and assistance to its residents, including pensions, unemployment support, and healthcare coverage.

Andorra's governance framework, while characterized by stability, is not without its challenges. As a small nation, the co-principality faces the task of balancing economic growth with environmental sustainability, preserving its cultural heritage while embracing globalization, and addressing the evolving needs and aspirations of its diverse population. The Andorran government continues to work towards finding the right balance and ensuring that policies and initiatives meet the expectations and aspirations of its residents.

In conclusion, contemporary Andorra is a co-principality that has experienced significant economic diversification, social changes, and unique governance arrangements. The co-principality has successfully transformed its economy from being predominantly agrarian and tourism-oriented to encompassing sectors such as finance, retail, technology, and trade. Andorra's society reflects a multicultural mix of residents from various backgrounds, contributing to a vibrant social fabric. The co-principality's governance structure, with its co-princes and parliamentary democracy, ensures a stable political system, while efforts are made to promote transparency, accountability, and good governance practices. Andorra's commitment to environmental preservation, social welfare, and international engagement further reflects its aspirations as a modern, forward-thinking nation.

The Cultural Heritage of Andorra: Preserving Tradition in a Modern World

Andorra's rich cultural heritage is a testament to its history, traditions, and the resilience of its people. This chapter explores the diverse elements of Andorran culture, highlighting the co-principality's efforts to preserve its traditions while embracing the opportunities and challenges of a modern world.

The official language of Andorra is Catalan, reflecting the co-principality's historical ties to Catalonia. Catalan is spoken by the majority of the population and serves as a key element of Andorran identity. Efforts have been made to promote and preserve the Catalan language through education, media, and cultural initiatives. The Andorran government supports Catalan-language publications, theater, music, and festivals as a means of fostering cultural pride and reinforcing a sense of identity among the population.

Religion has played a significant role in shaping Andorran culture. The co-principality has a predominantly Roman Catholic population, and religious traditions and practices are deeply ingrained in Andorran society. The influence of the Catholic Church can be seen in various aspects of Andorran life, including religious festivals, processions, and the architectural presence of churches and chapels. The co-princes, particularly the Bishop of Urgell, maintain a close relationship with the Church, and religious celebrations hold a prominent place in the annual calendar of events.

Andorra's cultural heritage is rich with folklore, legends, and traditional customs that have been passed down through generations. Folk dances, music, and costumes are important expressions of Andorran identity. The "contrapàs," a traditional dance performed in a circle, is a symbol of communal harmony and unity. Traditional costumes, characterized by embroidered details and regional variations, are worn during festivals and special occasions, showcasing the pride in Andorran heritage.

Festivals form an integral part of Andorran cultural life, providing opportunities for communal gatherings and the celebration of traditions. The co-principality boasts a calendar filled with vibrant and colorful festivals that reflect its religious, agricultural, and historical roots. The Carnival, the Feast of Saint John, the Feast of Our Lady of Meritxell, and the Andorra National Day (Diada Nacional) are among the most significant celebrations. These events showcase traditional music, dance performances, processions, and culinary specialties, offering a glimpse into Andorra's cultural tapestry.

Andorra's architectural heritage offers glimpses into its past and serves as a tangible reminder of its cultural roots. Romanesque churches, such as the Church of Santa Coloma and the Church of Sant Joan de Caselles, stand as testaments to medieval craftsmanship and religious devotion. The historical village of Ordino, with its well-preserved stone houses and narrow streets, offers a glimpse into traditional Andorran village life. The Casa de la Vall, the former seat of Andorra's political governance, is an iconic building that represents the co-principality's historical institutions.

Andorra has made significant efforts to preserve and showcase its cultural heritage through various museums and cultural institutions. The National Automobile Museum displays a collection of vintage cars, providing insights into the development of transportation. The Casa Rull Museum offers a glimpse into Andorra's rural past, showcasing traditional Andorran interiors and artifacts. The Postal Museum and the Comic Museum highlight different aspects of Andorran history and cultural expression. These institutions contribute to the preservation and promotion of Andorra's cultural heritage, offering educational and immersive experiences for visitors and locals alike.

Andorra has a long tradition of skilled craftsmanship, with artisans specializing in various traditional crafts. Wood carving, ceramics, and textiles are among the notable artisanal skills in Andorra. Local artisans create intricately carved wooden sculptures, decorative objects, and furniture, showcasing their craftsmanship and artistic talent. Ceramics workshops produce pottery and ceramic pieces, often inspired by Andorran nature and traditional motifs. Textile artisans weave fabrics, creating unique patterns and designs that reflect Andorra's cultural heritage.

Efforts to preserve traditional crafts are evident in the promotion of artisanal markets and the support provided to local artisans. These initiatives not only help sustain traditional skills but also contribute to the preservation of Andorra's cultural identity and provide economic opportunities for artisans.

Andorra recognizes the importance of cultural education and raising awareness about its heritage among the younger generation. The co-principality's educational system incorporates cultural studies and heritage preservation into the curriculum. Students learn about Andorran history, traditions, and folklore, fostering a sense of pride and understanding of their cultural roots. Cultural organizations and associations also play a vital role in promoting cultural awareness through exhibitions, workshops, and educational initiatives.

Preserving cultural heritage in a rapidly changing world presents challenges for Andorra. The influences of globalization, technological advancements, and shifting demographics can impact traditional practices and values. Balancing the preservation of cultural heritage with the demands of a modern society requires careful consideration and adaptability.

Andorra's commitment to preserving its cultural heritage is reflected in ongoing efforts to document, protect, and promote its traditions. The co-principality continues to invest in cultural infrastructure, supporting the renovation of historical sites and the development of cultural spaces. Collaborations with international organizations and neighboring countries also contribute to the exchange of cultural experiences and knowledge.

Looking ahead, the co-principality of Andorra recognizes the importance of embracing cultural heritage as a driver of sustainable tourism, economic growth, and social cohesion. By fostering an environment that values and promotes cultural preservation, Andorra aims to ensure that its unique traditions and heritage continue to thrive in the modern world.

In conclusion, Andorra's cultural heritage is a source of pride and identity for its people. From language and folklore to festivals, architecture, and traditional crafts, Andorra's cultural heritage is a vibrant tapestry that reflects its historical, religious, and social roots. The co-principality's commitment to preserving its cultural traditions, coupled with ongoing efforts to raise awareness and support cultural initiatives, paves the way for the continued celebration and transmission of Andorra's rich heritage in the face of modern challenges.

Andorra: A Country of the Past and the Future

Andorra, a small co-principality nestled in the Pyrenees Mountains, is a country that beautifully bridges the gap between its rich historical past and its aspirations for the future. This chapter delves into the co-principality's unique position, examining how its historical legacy shapes its present identity and exploring the opportunities and challenges it faces as it looks toward the future.

Andorra's historical legacy is an essential part of its identity. From its origins as a Roman settlement to its emergence as a sovereign state in the Middle Ages, the co-principality's history has shaped its institutions, culture, and social fabric. The co-princes, representing the spiritual and temporal powers, have played a central role in Andorra's governance for centuries. The enduring influence of the Catholic Church, the co-princes' unique partnership, and the preservation of ancient traditions are all hallmarks of Andorra's historical heritage.

Andorra's commitment to preserving its traditions and cultural heritage is remarkable. Despite the challenges of globalization and modernization, the co-principality has remained steadfast in safeguarding its linguistic, religious, and artistic traditions. The promotion of the Catalan language, the preservation of Romanesque architecture, and the celebration of traditional festivals are all testimonies to Andorra's dedication to its past. Cultural institutions, museums, and educational programs contribute to raising awareness and instilling a sense of pride in Andorran heritage among the population.

Andorra's natural beauty and its strategic location between France and Spain have positioned it as a thriving tourism destination. The co-principality attracts visitors from around the world, particularly those seeking outdoor activities such as skiing, hiking, and mountain biking. The development of modern infrastructure, including ski resorts, hotels, and entertainment facilities, has enhanced the tourism experience. Andorra's ability to balance tourism development with environmental preservation has allowed it to maintain its allure as a sustainable destination.

Andorra's economy has evolved significantly over the years, transitioning from an agrarian society to a diversified economy. While agriculture and tourism remain important sectors, the co-principality has expanded into finance, trade, retail, and technology. The favorable tax environment, coupled with its location within the European market, has attracted foreign investment and fostered economic growth. Andorra's ability to adapt to changing economic trends and embrace innovation positions it well for future development.

Andorra's commitment to environmental stewardship is evident in its efforts to protect its pristine natural landscapes. The co-principality has implemented sustainable practices, such as eco-friendly tourism initiatives, waste management programs, and the preservation of biodiversity. Andorra recognizes the importance of balancing economic development with environmental conservation to ensure the long-term sustainability of its natural resources.

While Andorra has achieved remarkable progress, it also faces challenges and opportunities as it looks toward the future. The co-principality must navigate the complexities of globalization, ensuring that its cultural heritage and traditions remain strong amidst changing societal dynamics. Striking a balance between economic growth and environmental sustainability is a continual challenge. Andorra also faces the task of diversifying its economy further, expanding beyond tourism and finance to create opportunities for its growing population.

Looking ahead, Andorra has several opportunities to seize. Its location as a crossroads between France and Spain offers possibilities for increased collaboration, trade, and cultural exchange. Technological advancements provide avenues for innovation and the development of a knowledge-based economy. Andorra's commitment to education, research, and technology initiatives positions it to harness these opportunities and propel its future growth.

In conclusion, Andorra is a country that cherishes its historical past while embracing the possibilities of the future. The co-principality's unique blend of history, tradition, and aspirations sets it apart on the global stage. Andorra's commitment to preserving its cultural heritage, fostering sustainable tourism, and diversifying its economy reflects its resilience and adaptability.

Thank you for taking the time to delve into the fascinating history and unique features of Andorra through this book. We hope that the chapters have provided you with a comprehensive understanding of Andorra's past, present, and future.

Your support and engagement as a reader mean a great deal to us, and we would be grateful if you could leave a positive review or share your thoughts on this book. Your feedback will not only help us improve our work but also encourage other readers to explore the captivating world of Andorra.

Once again, thank you for joining us on this journey through the captivating story of Andorra. We look forward to hearing your thoughts and welcoming you to future literary adventures.

Printed in Great Britain
by Amazon